221

Camdean School

Item no.   00881

KU-376-237

# of Jericho

Story by Penny Frank
Illustrated by Tony Morris

THE LION
STORY BIBLE

12

OXFORD · BATAVIA · SYDNEY

The Bible tells us how God chose the Israelites to be his special people. He made them a promise that he would always love and care for them. But they must obey him.

God had rescued the Israelites from the land of Egypt. He had brought them to a new land called Canaan. It was a land where plants grew well and there was plenty to eat.

God had chosen a new leader for his people — a man called Joshua. He would take the Israelites into the promised land.

You can find this story in your own Bible, in Joshua, chapters 2 to 6.

Copyright © 1986 Lion Publishing

Published by
Lion Publishing plc
Sandy Lane West, Littlemore, Oxford, England
ISBN 0 85648 737 6
Lion Publishing Corporation
1705 Hubbard Avenue, Batavia,
Illinois 60510, USA
ISBN 0 85648 737 6
Albatross Books Pty Ltd
PO Box 320, Sutherland, NSW 2232, Australia
ISBN 0 86760 521 9

First edition 1986
Reprinted 1987, 1988

All rights reserved

Printed in Yugoslavia
Bound in Great Britain

**British Library Cataloguing in
Publication Data**

Frank, Penny
 The battle of Jericho. — (The Lion
Story Bible: 12)
1. Joshua — Juvenile literature
2. Bible stories, English — O.T. Joshua
I. Title   II. Morris, Tony,
1938 Aug. 2 —
222'20924   BS580/7

ISBN 0-85648-737-6

**Library of Congress Cataloging in
Publication Data**

Frank, Penny.
 The battle of Jericho.
(The Lion Story Bible: 12)
1. Bible stories. English — O.T. Joshua.
2. Jericho–History–Siege. ca. 1400
3. C. –Jouvenile literature (1. Jericho–
History–Siege. ca. 1400 B.C. 2. Joshua
(Biblicat figure) 3. Bible stories–O.T.)
I. Title. II. Morris, Tony. ill. III. Series:
Frank, Penny. Lion Story Bible: 12.
BS551.2.F66 1986   22'209505
85-24094
ISBN 0-85648-737-6

The Israelites were camping by the River
Jordan. On the other side of the river
was the land of Canaan. God had
promised long ago that the Israelites
would live in this land.

They had spent many years in the
desert. At last the promised land was in
sight.

God said to Joshua, the leader, 'I promise to give you and your people the whole land of Canaan if you obey me.

'I shall be with you, just as I was with Moses,' God said, 'so there is no need to be afraid. I shall never leave you on your own.'

Joshua was glad that God had spoken to him. He knew they would have to fight the people who already lived in the land.

Joshua said to the Israelites, 'Come and get ready. We are going into the new land.'

The Israelites were very excited. They began to pack up their tents.

Joshua chose two men to spy out the land.

'We will get ready by the river here,' he said. 'You two must go over and find out about that big city called Jericho. We must fight our first battle there.'

The two men crossed the river to the new land of Canaan. They found the city of Jericho. It had high walls and strong gates. They met a woman called Rahab, who lived in a house in the city walls.

When the king of Jericho sent soldiers to catch the men, Rahab hid them under a pile of flax on the flat roof.

'I have heard of the wonderful things your God has done,' Rahab said. 'Please promise me that I will be safe when you fight against this city.'

The men promised, and after dark Rahab helped them to escape. Then they went back to Joshua.

The people were all ready to cross the river. There was no bridge, and they had no boats.

The men who carried the special box which held God's laws went first. It was covered in gold and it shone in the sun.

As they stepped into the river, the water stopped flowing. The men stood in the middle with the box. The people walked across the river on dry ground.

12

They were in Canaan at last! The
Israelites said 'Thank you' to God for
bringing them safely through the river.

Joshua told them to pick up twelve
large stones from the river.

They piled up the stones. Joshua said,
'Now everyone who comes past here will
point to these stones. They will
remember how God brought you into
this new land.'

Joshua and the Israelites walked towards Jericho. The city walls were high and the gates were locked. All the people were inside.

'I will give you this city,' said God. 'But it will take seven days to win the battle.

14

'Every day for six days you must walk once right around the city. Seven priests, blowing their trumpets, will walk in front of my special box. The soldiers who follow must keep quiet. On the seventh day you must walk around the city seven times. Then the people can shout, and the city will be yours.'

Joshua did just as God had told him. Each day they walked once around Jericho. All the people watched them from the city walls.

First came the men with the trumpets. What a noise they made!

Then came the men with the special box.

Then came the rest of the Israelites. They were silent.

On the seventh day the Israelites walked around Jericho seven times.

The people in Jericho felt suddenly afraid. They could not understand what Joshua's army was doing.

Then, suddenly, Joshua told the Israelites to shout. They were really glad. They had been silent for so long.

And, when they shouted, the city walls of Jericho fell down!

The Israelites marched in and took the city, just as God had said.

'Go and keep your promise to rescue Rahab, because she helped you,' Joshua told them. 'Then we must destroy the city.'

The Israelites had won their first battle in the land God had promised to them.

Joshua knew that they must go on
trusting God.

'There will be many more battles to
fight,' he said, 'before the land will
belong to us. But God has promised that
he will always be with us.'

The Lion Story Bible is made up of 52 individual stories for young readers, building up an understanding of the Bible as one story — God's story — a story for all time and all people.

The Old Testament section (numbers 1–30) tells the story of a great nation — God's chosen people, the Israelites — and God's love and care for them through good times and bad. The stories are about people who knew and trusted God. From this nation came one special person, Jesus Christ, sent by God to save all people everywhere.

The stories told in *The battle of Jericho* come from the Old Testament book of Joshua, chapters 2–6. The battle itself is in chapters 5 and 6.

God had promised to give his people the land of Canaan to live in. The first great victory showed that this did not depend on anything they did themselves. They had only to do as God said, and to trust him.

The next story in this series is number 13: *Gideon fights for God*. The Israelites have settled in their new land but they are under attack. Once again God sends a champion to rescue them.